...ne

...smine Mans's talent
...re than that, though,
...of love in a life from
childhood to adulthood and all the way back home. . . . You are
carrying in your hands a black woman's heart."

—Jericho Brown,
author of Pulitzer Prize winner *The Tradition*

"Mans takes up the tools of Gwendolyn Brooks and Sonia Sanchez
into her good hands and chisels us an urgent and grand work, proving
why she's the favorite poet of all the girls in the back of the bus."

—Danez Smith, author of National Book Award finalist
Don't Call Us Dead

"This book is a haven for all the Black daughters out there hop-
ing to make sense of the power and powerlessness in their bod-
ies, the connection to others' bodies, and the moments o...
everyday life that comprise so much of our identities."

—Morgan Jerkin...
New York Times bestselling author of *This Will Be My Undoing*

"Each poem is a meditation on a moment, a memory, and a...
history that guides the reader through the experience of Bla...
womanhood in a way I've not experienced before. These po...
both explode and glimmer on the page. They demand...
read, to be shared, to be revisited time and time again."...

—Clint...
author of NAACP Image Award finalist *Counting*...

"Writing in surefooted verse, Mans refuses to allow our stories to be misunderstood; she needs the world to get it for once. . . . So if you find yourself lost in a past that predates you or a city that erased you, these poems promise to look for you—damn where you been. They will welcome you home and fix you a plate, quietly, like any mother would."

—Dr. Alysia Nicole Harris, Pushcart-nominated author of *How Much We Must Have Looked Like Stars to Stars*

"The collection is so steeped with tenderness, it feels intimate and wholly relatable—we hear our mother's warnings, our grandmother's wisdom, and our lover's regret beneath her words. This is a phenomenal debut."

—Maisy Card, author of *These Ghosts Are Family*

BLACK GIRL, CALL HOME

(973)

BLACK GIRL, CALL HOME

JASMINE MANS

BERKLEY

NEW YORK

BERKLEY
An imprint of Penguin Random House LLC
penguinrandomhouse.com

Copyright © 2021 by Jasmine Mans
Penguin Random House supports copyright. Copyright fuels creativity,
encourages diverse voices, promotes free speech, and creates a vibrant culture.
Thank you for buying an authorized edition of this book and for complying
with copyright laws by not reproducing, scanning, or distributing any part of
it in any form without permission. You are supporting writers and allowing
Penguin Random House to continue to publish books for every reader.

BERKLEY and the BERKLEY & B colophon are registered trademarks of
Penguin Random House LLC.

Library of Congress Cataloging-in-Publication Data

Names: Mans, Jasmine, author.
Title: Black girl, call home / Jasmine Mans.
Description: First edition. | New York: Berkley, 2021. | Includes
bibliographical references.
Identifiers: LCCN 2020036788 (print) | LCCN 2020036789 (ebook) | ISBN
9780593197141 (trade paperback) | ISBN 9780593197158 (ebook)
Subjects: LCSH: Coming of age—Poetry. | LCGFT: Poetry.
Classification: LCC PS3613.A569 B57 2021 (print) | LCC PS3613.A569
(ebook) | DDC 811/.6—dc23
LC record available at https://lccn.loc.gov/2020036788
LC ebook record available at https://lccn.loc.gov/2020036789

First Edition: March 2021

Printed in the United States of America
1 3 5 7 9 10 8 6 4 2

Cover image: *Adeline in Barrettes* © Micaiah Carter
Cover design by Dominique Jones
Book design by Kristin del Rosario

For Mommy and Nana

Bald-headed cabbage patch
ain't got no hair in the back.
Bald-headed skittle diddle
ain't got no hair in the middle[1]

---

1. Black girl rhyme, author unknown.

I Ain't Gon' Be Bald-Headed No More

I wore these braids for two
whoooole months, and tonight
Momma gonna wash my hair
when she gets off work at 7 p.m.

It's longer than it was before,
and when I wear it out at school,
the rest of the girls
won't call me bald-headed
no more.

Imma be pretty,
as soon as momma gets home
from work.

Momma Has a Hair Salon in the Kitchen

Wash
Barrettes
Twists
Crisscross
Braids
Beads
Cornrows
Wooden brush
Edges
Silk scarf
Nappy
Kitchen
Beady beads
4c
Coil
Ouch
SuperGrow
Straighten
Burn
Breakage
Drip dry
Split
Crunch
Grow
Cut
4a
Yakky

Bundle
Bleach
Chop
Short
Dye
Curl
Slick
Toothbrush
Damage
Afro
Roller set
Shrinking
Ugly
Long
Thin
Thinning
Thinner
Weave
Heat
Press
Hot comb
No edges
Toothbrush
Nigga naps
Sheen
Spritz
Dryer
"Hold ya head still!"
Deep conditioning
Pretty

Bleach
Vaseline
Shrunk
Burn
Breakage
"Don't make me pop you!"
Scalp
Fine
Just for Me
Poison
Natural
Pressed
Dry
Damage
Edges
Trim
"Be still"
"Hold your ear"

Momma prays
like she's talking over God,
and if God were to talk back
she wouldn't even hear Him.

That Was Her Way of Showing God

We didn't go to church on Sundays,
but my mother cleaned
the whole house.

Wiped from behind the toilet—
to inside of the oven.
That was her way
of honoring God.

Separating cloth
by color,
making sure
nothing bled,
onto anything else,
stretching pork
across seven days,
because even poverty
knows ritual.

Baptizing Black babies
in bathtubs
of hand-me-down water,
one, after
another.
A poor woman's tradition,
but of its own abundance.

That was her way of showing God
that she had a servant's heart,
that she was a good woman,
with all of the little
she had.

Macaroni and Cheese

"Macaroni and cheese,"
my mother says,
". . . is all about pattern,"
and how well
you can harden the edges
without burning them.

Ma could count a teaspoon
with the lines on her palms,
could measure an ocean
and tell you how long it would take
to bring it to a slow boil.

She'd say
the women in our family
grated their own cheeses,
bought their greens fresh
from the harvest farm,
and made sure the babies ate them
for a good bowel movement.

She wouldn't let us lick
the whole batter,
but gave us the spoon.
She could remember Easter
when the rest of the family
forgot God.

She'd say
"You'll sit there until
you finish your plate."
Thought waste was the worst sin.
Told us about all the starving kids
in Africa who'd give anything
for her meat loaf.

She didn't let things go bad.
She didn't let anything spoil
in her refrigerator.

I know grace and mercy was raised
by the same single mother.

We Host These Variables

We try to leverage language as a means to a truth. We learn, on our paths, perhaps, that certain stories have no language, nor require one. There's something I want to honor here. I want to honor the silent story, the emotions unaccompanied by human language. I want to honor the weight of the stillness. I want to honor the silent ceremony between mother and daughter. A ceremony of blood and becoming. Because, I know, we exist with a heavy and stubborn resemblance. I know the distance between mother and daughter. How we are many burned bridges, as well as, a wealth of brick and clay, ready to be made anew from everything unmade of us. I am learning my mother's song, staring into her silence, as it stares back at me. Wondering of its depth, and wandering through it. I don't know all of her pain, or if it can be held with two hands. But she looks back at me, with girlish eyes, wanting to be remembered for something I do not recognize her as. Daughters have questions for their mothers, questions made up of no words; we host these variables. A woman stretched her body for me, and I have no words to describe her in wholeness, but without shame, I want you to know her. My mother.

Speak to Me of My Mother, Who Was She

Tell me about the girl
my mother was,
before she traded in
all her girl
to be my mother.

What did she smell like?
How many friends did she have,
before she had no room?

Before I took up so much
space in her prayers,
who did she pray for?

B'Nai's Three Babies

B'Nai had three children.
C-sections with all three,
two boys and one girl.

Each of them
would've stayed inside her
and she would've let them
because she loved them babies
that kinda way.

They gave her gas,
chest pains,
and sat right on her bladder,
but they were *her* babies.

Antione was the first,
the one that would usher her
into motherhood.
He was the baby
that made Tyrone
marry B'Nai.
The one she'd dress up
and flaunt around.

The baby that every aunty
had a naked picture of.

He was the baby
that got Aunty
off drugs. She tells
folks that God sent
Antione to save her,
and she let him.

Jasmine was the second baby,
delivered in St. Michael's Hospital,
screamed when she was born
like all babies do, but didn't stop,
a colic baby.

Cried like she already knew
how much pain
the world had in it.
Jasmine sent B'Nai
into a tired depression.
She gave up sleep
for that little girl,
and her job at the bank.

Said that she didn't have time
to make anything else
of her hands, but cradle.

Sometimes the neighbors
would come over
and hold the baby.

These women knew
what it was like
to have three babies,
a working husband,
and to be left all alone
with the smallness.

LT was the last baby,
named after Tyrone,
the one they couldn't afford,
and truthfully,
they couldn't afford any of them.

Tyrone got his second job
when LT was born,
worked all seven days
out of the week,
because that's what men
are supposed to do.

LT was the biggest
and still is,
weighed ten pounds,
when he was born.

B'Nai's favorite baby,
the one that loves his momma,
has his nana's eyes,
a happy baby.

The one
she fed turkey legs,
and pork bacon to.
The baby that sucked the chicken bone.

The one she'd hold on to
the longest.
The lightest, and most sensitive
out of the three.

There were three babies,
and a woman stumbling
into motherhood.

No money,
and an apartment
in Newark.

She learned how to cook
with those children,
learned what spaghetti
and meat loaf could do.

She prayed to God
for her babies
that they'd learn
the vocabulary
she didn't have.

Prayed to God,
for him to spare her three
Black babies, when the plague came.

Because she was their momma,
and she was gonna do right
by each of them.

Period

Mothers teach their daughters
how to hide the blood,
how to wash out the stains upon arrival.

To pretend like the blood isn't there, or theirs.
Mothers teach their daughters
to make sure the blood doesn't have an odor.

To never let the stench rise.
Mothers teach their daughters
to be misleading about the amount
of blood. And the weight it adds to the body.

Mothers teach their daughters to never bleed
out. To not use the blood as an excuse, even
when the blood
is the only
excuse.

I resent my mother
for things she has sacrificed
on my behalf.

Treat Her Right, While She's Still Here

When I hang up
on my mother,
Sabrina says,

"Must be nice.
"I never had a mother
to hang up on.
I wasn't old enough
to have a cell phone,
or an attitude,
when my mother died."

Before my mother knew
I was a lesbian,
she prepared me
to be a man's wife.

Momma Said Dyke at the Kitchen Table

Momma said,
so you gonna be a dyke now?

As if she meant to say,
didn't I raise you better than that,
don't you know
I ain't raise no dyke,
don't you know
you too pretty to be a dyke?

Why you gonna embarrass us like this,
you scared no man gonna love you,
you scared of men,
some mannnnnnn hurt you,
who hurt you?

Momma said,
so you gonna be a dyke now?

As if she meant to say,
don't you know
how hard it already is
for women like us,
why you gonna go
and make it harder on yourself?

I don't want you in that kind of pain,
this world ain't sweet on those kinds of women,
I don't want another reason to be scared for you.

Momma said,
so you gonna be a dyke now?

As if she meant to say,
I'm scared for you.

The First Time the Black Girl Calls
Her Mother a Bitch

This is the moment
the Black girl unmothers herself,
when she refers to her momma
as bitch, and the word
settles in her mouth,
like a razor under
her childish tongue.

She will run away wearing
her womanhood, like a loose pair
of heels. Her breasts will sit up higher
than they were.

She will stand nosey
and act bigger than herself.

In this part of the story
she doesn't have a mother,

But she does,
she always will.

Grits: 1967

Nana's kitchen
is as old as the Civil Rights Movement,
sometimes she can't remember
which came first,
the grits,
or the riots.

Birmingham

Momma said the bomb
wasn't meant for me.
I think it was meant for Pastor Martin
because he be havin' them dreams.

Maybe those white men didn't know
that little Black girls

we be goin' to church too,
and we be foldin' our hands,
praying and we be taking communion
just like their daughters do.

Maybe if I wore my church shoes
the bad men would've never came for me.
I knew they matched my dress
but they always just be hurtin' my feet.

I be thinkin', did God christen the bombs
that exploded my flesh into sacrifice?

And do anybody be hearin'
those sacrificial scriptures,
spoken in tongues,
claiming Christ,
before everything went boom?
Before the smoke

and rubble
baptized these collapsing bones?

Maybe if they knew,
we were like the most beautiful flowers,
right before the wind and dirt
began playing tug-of-war
with the delicates
of our petals.

Momma said,
it only took one man
to die for the sins
of this entire world,
so how did that man
let this church tremble
on my soul?

And I don't remember
there being enough holy water
to stop the smoke,
or to calm the burning.

Momma said,
some heartbreaks just be too hard
to swallow at communion,
some serpents
just be finding salvation
in baptismal pools,

some church mice
just be screaming
America's dirty little secrets.

Momma said
some deaths,
just be too black,
and too white
to be labeled holy,

Some sacrifice comes without permission,
Some sacrifice comes without fair warning,

God can't always protect you
from the boogie man,
so some baby girls will reach the pearly gates
and won't be tall enough to turn the handle.

Momma said,
some men . . .
some men
will just be too guilty to claim innocence
with their own Christ.

But what did . . . what did I do?
I never wanted to play with the white girls.
I—I never asked for integration;
I wanted roller skates—
an extra piece of cake, after dinnertime.

Sometimes I just be thinking,
maybe God was too busy
trying to protect Martin
to think about us,
I ain't never ask
for that man's dream.

But momma . . .
momma be sayin'
that his dream
just been askin'
for me.

South 14th Street:
Nana's House Smells Like Cigarettes

Nana's house still smells
like cigarettes.

Today,
Nana got open heart surgery
she still drinks Pepsis,
she still smokes,
she's still strong.

But her heart
don't trust her,
well,
not like it used to.

Nana smells like Newports,
it reminds us
that things caught smoke,
but never did they catch fire.

South 14th Street: The Attic Window

From "Waiting"

My grandfather died
in bed with my nana.

She said she saw
His soul soar
right out of their attic window.

He left his body
in that bed to remind her,
that even without breath
she could still wake up
to him.

She said, he left silently
didn't want to wake her up
out her sleep as he got ready
to leave.

Kissed her on the cheek,
gathered himself
at the foot of the bed
and didn't take anything
with him,
not even her smile.

South 14th Street: For Sale

Nana is selling the house,
the one on South 14th Street,
off of Clinton Ave.
The house she was married in,
the olive house
with the hunter green trim,
the house with the uneven
driveway, that skins the chin
of every car that tries to pull up,
even the nice ones.

The wood is just rotten, the pipes
need replacing, and Nana, she's just too old
to maintain it all. The neighbors
ain't like they were back in the day.

Things have changed
since poppa died,
and it's different
without no one 'round
to take out the trash
and to shovel
the steps.

At Aunt Kawee's House in Oklahoma

She woke up out of her
sleep, saw them, and
yelled to those angels
from the bottom of her
throat!

"Get away from that bed!"

And those angels left,
empty-handed,
they left.

"And her voice was a drowning piano."

Blame

I blame my father
for things he cannot control.

I blame my father
for things he can control
but chooses not to.

I've seen my mother
with a broken heart
before.

I blame my father
for all of my mother's
broken hearts.

The Thing That Made Him My Father

I've never seen my father cry,
or speak of his mother's death.
He doesn't talk about his brother,
the one that passed away.

He doesn't talk
about what he remembers
of his first father,
or his second.

He doesn't speak of the story
that made him my father,
or a man.

Because I Am a Woman Now

Nana may have cancer,
and I'm looking for my mother
to tell me that it'll be okay,
that there is no such thing as cancer,
that Nana is stronger than cancer,
that cancer has no place in our family,
or in her body, that we know prayers stronger
than cancer. But she won't say those things
because I am a woman now.

So she says . . .

"We'll see,
we don't know,
but we'll see."

Nana's heart sits between two cancers.
The left and right lung.

I have reason to believe
God made dandelions
and metaphors
on the same day.

Nerf Guns: Christmas 2019, Tulsa

Today, at age twenty-eight, I played with my first Nerf
gun. First, watching as children old enough to be my
own nieces and nephews made a merry-go-round of
themselves, trotting from kitchen to living room with
plastic guns, as big as their own torsos. Shooting off
bullets made of Styrofoam. The only way a bullet
becomes laughter is when it plays pretend in its own
foam shadow.

These babies, old enough to still be babies, aim at each
other, screaming "I killed you, you're dead." The
Christmas nostalgia of newly unwrapped toys, still
smelling of plastic and not yet like home, made me
think about how my father never bought us "fun toys."
Toys that allowed us to play pretend with words like
"murder" and "dead" weren't allowed at home. Maybe,
for my father, these words were as triggering as the
trigger itself. We weren't allowed to play dead with our
toys, or with one another. My father knew death too
well to let us mimic it. Or, maybe death mimicked us
too well for him to allow its "pretend" in his house.

But the day after Christmas, I watched as Walter
begged his dad to get his Nerf from the car. With gun
and ammunition in hand, he and his cousins turned
their Pop-Pop's house into a war zone, a playground.
And their toy guns were more toy than gun. I joined in, to

help the girls. Shooting plastic foam at the baby bodies of five-year-old boys, who giggled during their play deaths. Who will live a decade before understanding the metaphors of their toys.

And for a few moments, I wrapped myself in that joy. The joy that nothing spilled of them but the sound of their own silly. These guns, orange and gray, chambers filled with Styrofoam, only in the hands of five-year-olds, can make death, not death at all.

Your little sister thinks
your blood was the dye
that turned every rose
red.

All Them Bags

A dead boy threw a rock at my window.
He asked me where all the flowers from his
memorial went and where'd they put all the
teddy bears tied up to the fence after the rain
stopped. If the Jackie Robinson
Little League team was still undefeated, and if his
mother and sister still walk from the grocery
store on Lyons and Chancellor Ave. every
Monday
and if it's hard for them to
carry all those bags
without him.

I know some Black boys stand outside all day,
simply because no one is looking for them.

I sought you
like a prisoner's sunlight
yesterday.

All Too Normal

All too normal
how we let our boys go,

and try to find them
after they're gone,
and the longing.

All too normal
the tremor of longing,

and how it fits
uncomfortably

in our everythings,
everywhere.

All too normal
how we don't
know

what we . . .

. . . until it's . . .

and the skin,
the skin they
be wearing.

All too normal
how it stays so perfect,

for the morning,
and mourning after.

And Jay-Z Says "We've Moved Past Kneeling"

If we past kneeling,
How come we ain't past dying?

Black Son

After Alysia Harris on Sean Bell

How do you tell a woman
that raising a Black son
isn't some type of inside joke
crafted by God
and some white man?

Can you prove to me
they are not in Heaven
snickering at the soul
of a single parent mother
dressing her son
for graduation,
hoping he can make it
across the stage,
down the aisle, or off
the balcony
quick enough to not
get caught, in his skin,
at the wrong time?

I've touched the bellies of women
who will look you in the eyes
like a bluebird
awakening to a holocaust
and whisper . . .

"I am just afraid
to raise a Black son."

A Black boy
is just a trembling soul
suffocating
in a fabric that always
seemed to make you itch
around the neck.

The tag that makes you
scratch around your noose
collar.

How can you tell a mother
holding her son
in the delivery room.
Praying that his skin
doesn't get any darker.

Hoping it'll stay
as light and deceiving
as a sunrise in the ghetto,
that her son isn't
some white man's pit stop.

That her son's body
isn't a chamber
for some bigot to store

his sin and Southern accent in,
that her son isn't some colored toy
for the rich blue-eyed boys.

Can you tell her
her son's penis isn't dark enough
to be considered rape
in the Confederate states.

"I am just afraid to raise a Black son."

Who will spend
the rest of his life
praying for a melody,
or a melanin
safe enough to scream in,
a son who has to be a martyr
for a war he never asked for.

The Repass: Our Own Restaurant

The women will bring
macaroni and cheese
to the funeral,

fried chicken,
peach cobbler,
potato salad,

and dinner rolls
that come wholesale
at Costco.

A mourning family
shouldn't have to cook
for themselves.

You never
let a mother in sorrow
fix her own plate.

You make her a plate first,
give her extra gravy
on her mashed potatoes and chicken.

Stack her up a real good plate
that juices onto her hands,
a plate that sogs from the collards.

Turn the church basement
into a Black momma's
restaurant, let the children run,
scrambling themselves
between the tables.

Make the men
bring the extra folding chairs
from the storage closet,
tell Aunty that the Pepsis
are deep deep in the cooler.

Wait on her
give her a side of rum cake
take good care of her
like she be your favorite
customer.

Your Brother's Keeper

For NoMalice

Son, I had a dream
that I looked
in your brother's room
and he wasn't there,

that I told you to watch him
and you forgot about him.

But I'm sure
he went off

hid in the bushes,
under the bed,
in the cellar,

or somewhere far down
my knees are too brittle to find.

Chile, dinner is in two hours,
we got collard greens,
extra fish,
we gon' eat well tonight.

Grab this bag for
me, put your shoes
away, wash up for

dinner, got all that
dirt all over your
hands, whatchu
been doin',

go get your brother,
bring him to me.

I had a dream that you
pawned him off, led
him astray, told him
that you'd be back,
and left his
bones shivering
in the wild.

Did you leave him for dead?

Did you not think to bring
his bones back to me, to
shove them in your closet, or
in the trunk of your car?

How much was he worth,
you sold him for cheap,
didn't you?

Did you sell his voice
to some blues beat that
a nigga remixed in his

mother's basement to
the smell of reefer, and
the insides of some
faceless girl?

Don't remember
the last dirt road
you scattered his parts
on?

Can you remember
if you left the receipt
for his skull in your pants pocket,
or in the trash of the man
who gave it to you?

Boy, I had a dream
you left your brother
on the belly of an
unfamiliar road
with no change in his
front pocket to tell his momma
he won't make it home
in time for supper.

Did you, at least, send him
off on a full stomach,
like I taught you?

I Know You Didn't Mean to Kill Him:
An Excerpt

Could never tell the difference
between the mother of the murdered
and the mother of the murderer,

both shook in solemn,

both their eyes
and memory
blue in tint,

both lost their grips
when they lost their sons,

developed a stutter
in their palms,

one became scared
of her shadow,
while the other,
just became one.

Unwelcome

He died
as if
God
thought
he
outstayed
the welcome
in his own skin.

The Boys on Broad Street Play With Coins

Yesterday, I spent some time hanging out with a friend visiting from Milwaukee. His flight was leaving from LaGuardia at 7 p.m. and we had some time to kill.

We walked down Newark's Broad St. at what felt like three in the afternoon, not because of the sun, or the weather, but because high school students were everywhere. They were out of school, absorbing that precious time between the last ring of the school bell and the two hours before their mothers start looking for them. For students, these are crucial, and political moments.

Some will immediately tackle their responsibilities, picking up their siblings from neighboring schools. Others will indulge in extracurricular activities, like basketball and debate. And many, many will kick it.

While kicking it, these students will indulge in their own standards of hip-hop, culture, and politics. I won't generalize the complexities of the "after-school narrative" because these kids talk about what they've seen and what they'll eventually unsee.

That day, a different conversation happened. Black boys stood in a broken circle, cypher-like. All in uniforms, backpacks armored to their spines. Haircuts that only

Black boys can have, and wearing their mandatory black school shoes.

"If I had to be raped or be a rapist, I'd be a rapist!" A Black boy said aloud. The most intriguing thing was his certainty.

It is October 2018, and Bill Cosby has been arrested on multiple counts of rape. The #MeToo Movement has shaken both Hollywood and politics to its core. Rape is talked about everywhere as horror story and cultural banter alike.

And in Newark, on Broad Street, at what felt like three in the afternoon, this is how Black boys projected the culture they are inheriting onto one another. The raped, or rapist. This is what they have come back with, to their tribe of Black boys. They don't know that their own mothers and sisters sit in the metaphors of their childish ignorance.

I didn't say anything. Cowardly and unwelcomed, we slowly passed them on Broad Street. Shocked, but unbrave in our ability to reach them, or offer objection.

24 Hours After It Happens

Are you listening? / Can I read you these instructions? /
You can feel free to stop me if I am speaking too fast. /
Can you place your sheets in this plastic bag and hand it
back to me? / Next, can I swab your cheek for saliva?
It'll be quick. / Can you urinate in this cup? If you don't
have to urinate it's okay, I'll leave it here for when you're
ready. / Was there any blood? / Where? / I would like
you to run this comb through your hair for DNA, can you
do that? / Can I see your right hand, okay, now your
left. / Have you finished filling out all of your
documentation? / Can I have your signature here,
please? Did you know him? Do you know his number?
What about his Instagram? Facebook? / Where did it
happen? / Did he leave anything? Let me know if this is
too much for you and we can stop at any moment.

We can't make promises like that,

but we'll do our best.

Secrets

The day I died,
I didn't tell
my body.

Traffick

When the girls reach
the border,

they will stand
in staggering
shades of brown.

Pronouncing their names
through tired lips.

Their accents will lay
heavy on their tongues,
like yeast,
in protest
of its own vacancy.

They will hold themselves,
bellies already filled,
with a swelling
that only emptiness
can conjure.

They will claim
each other as kin
to honor the horror,
or, to at least,

remember it was real,
—they weren't alone—and
were of many.

Their names are the first
things lost in the traffic,
the most hesitant to leave
but the first thing
dragged out
of the girl-
women.

Kanye's Black Aunties

For some reason
Black women
never give up
on men like you.

For we know
we made you,
and who are we
to just let
our sister's son
die?

Through the Wire

When you look
in the mirror
do you see the boy
with a jaw wired shut,

trying to sing his song
through locked teeth,

A mouth that won't
let him scream,
still trapped
in a car
he can't get
himself
out of.

Gravity to a God

Today, a boy wrote
his prayers
on a piece of paper,
and threw it
towards the sky,

when it fell to the ground,
he, then, made gravity his God.

Searching for a Feeling

How many white houses
did you walk in,
searching for your God?

Footnotes for Kanye

You look hungry,
like that girl don't make you
no fried chicken
or macaroni and cheese,
like she don't feel you on the inside,
like you haven't had a home-cooked meal
since your momma died.

You look like you lost the Psalm
in your own song
like you want to talk to God,
but you're afraid,
because y'all ain't spoke in so long.[2]

Do you tell your daughter about me,
how we were bittersweet,[3]

"To never mess with entertainers
because they always leave."[4]

"He'll get on

---

2. Kanye West, "Jesus Walks," *The College Dropout*, Roc-A-Fella Records, 2004.

3. Kanye West, "Bittersweet" (featuring John Mayer), *Graduation*, Roc-A-Fella Records, 2007.

4. Kanye West, "Homecoming," *Graduation*, Roc-A-Fella Records, 2007.

and he'll leave your ass
for a white girl."[5]

He'll give her your style,
your language,
your waist,
damn near try
to give her your face,
and somewhere
in his post-traumatic
twisted fantasy[6]
he'll make it all okay.
But what's the worth
in loving a man
who's lost his smile
anyway?

When Kim fucks up the lyrics
to *The College Dropout*[7]
like them white folks
used to fuck up your name,[8]
do you pretend not to notice?

5. Kanye West, "Homecoming," *Graduation*, Roc-A-Fella Records, 2007.

6. Kanye West, *My Beautiful Dark Twisted Fantasy*, Roc-A-Fella Records, 2010.

7. Kanye West, *The College Dropout*, Roc-A-Fella Records, 2004.

8. Kanye West, "Diamonds from Sierra Leone," *Late Registration*, Roc-A-Fella Records, 2005.

Do you regret the Marilyn Monroe
in your decision, and wish
you could've taken Billie Holiday
as your bride?

Do you ever want to run
back to your wedding day
and have it all over
on the South Side?

Do you wake up
in the middle of the night
and just think she wasn't the right girl
like maybe you should've found
one of them "I-like-art-type girls."[9]

Can you hear all the Black kids
calling your name?
Wondering why the boy
who rapped about his momma
getting arrested for the sit-ins
didn't sit in—[10]

Why he traded in his Nat Turner

9. Kanye West, "Blame Game," *My Beautiful Dark Twisted Fantasy*,
Roc-A-Fella Records, 2010.

10. Kanye West, "Never Let Me Down," *The College Dropout*, Roc-A-Fella
Records, 2004.

for Ralph Lauren?
Do you know
how many kids at the protest
had your sneakers on?
None of them.

Do you know how many
of your songs were played
at the protest?
All of them.

Could you hear
All of the Lights,[11]
the Flashing Lights,[12]
the New Slaves,[13]
the Runaways—
on their road to redemption
waiting for Malcolm West
to have the whole world at attention.[14]

Nigga, they got you quiet,

11. Kanye West, "All of the Lights," *My Beautiful Dark Twisted Fantasy*,
Roc-A-Fella Records, 2010.

12. Kanye West, "Flashing Lights," *Graduation*, Roc-A-Fella Records, 2007.

13. Kanye West, "New Slaves," *Yeezus*, Def Jam Records, 2013.

14. Kanye West, "Gorgeous," *My Beautiful Dark Twisted Fantasy*, Roc-A-Fella
Records, 2010.

"Like, how come only at awards shows—he riots."[15]

Maybe Yeezus was all talk.
Jesus never needed Adidas to walk.[16]
Why is he outlining sneakers
when the South Side is outlined in chalk?

Can someone go and find
the man who could make a diamond
with his own bare hands?[17]
We are looking for you.

Because these kids
still want to be just like you.
They want to rap
and make soul beats
just like you.[18]
Even though
you just not you.

---

15. "Taylor, Imma let you finish . . . but Beyoncé had one of the best videos of all time!" Kanye West to Taylor Swift during her acceptance speech for an award at the 2009 MTV Video Music Awards.

16. Kanye West, "Jesus Walks," *The College Dropout*, Roc-A-Fella Records, 2004.

17. Kanye West, "Diamonds from Sierra Leone," *Late Registration*, Roc-A-Fella Records, 2005.

18. Kanye West, "Homecoming," *Graduation*, Roc-A-Fella Records, 2007.

Even though you traded in
your spaceship[19]
to buy back your 40 acres
and a mule, purchased the plantation,
and master's daughters too.

Nigga, why you got these white folks
claiming you, like they built you,
like they made you,
like they polished you,
like they readied them a good nigga
for the picking,
like they got you for sale—
oh, how they love Kanye.
Let's put him all in front of the store[20]
like you their Black boy,
you forgot you Black, boy?
They got you lost in this world?[21]

You getting blackmailed for that white girl?[22]

19. Kanye West, "Spaceship," *The College Dropout*, Roc-A-Fella Records, 2004.

20. Kanye West, "Spaceship," *The College Dropout*, Roc-A-Fella Records, 2004.

21. Kanye West, "Lost in a World," *My Beautiful Dark Twisted Fantasy*,
Roc-A-Fella Records, 2010.

22. Kanye West, "Lost in a World," *My Beautiful Dark Twisted Fantasy*,
Roc-A-Fella Records, 2010.

You don't see how your lies is affecting me,
you don't see how our lives were supposed to be?

And I never let a nigga get that close to me,
and you ain't cracked up
to what you were supposed to be.[23]

I guess it's bittersweet poetry.[24]

---

23. Kanye West, "Bittersweet Poetry," *Russell Simmons Def Poetry*, HBO, 2006.

24. Kanye West, "Bittersweet Poetry," *Russell Simmons Def Poetry*, HBO, 2006.

Your God

We can't be together
for I believe in my God,
more than you do
your own.

3 O'clock in the Morning

You call,
at three in the morning.

I answer,
we are the only two,
in the world,
awake.

We talk,
like we discovered God
before everyone else
did.

I Watch Her Sleep

She is a night's reach.

I watch her sleep, and
everything around her
becomes sanctuary.

I wonder of the story she sleeps
in, and wish not of it in gray.
I begin to listen for parts of her
body that only speak in the
silence. The parts that only
speak through drip, and funk,
and murmur, and reach, and
wind. She hardens by morning,
as all women have to.

The sun crawls itself up
her sheets like a needy
child,
and she is, now, more
of Morning's than
of mine.

Laughing Sanctuaries

Your laugh is for sanctuaries,
and everything else
that holds God,
and an echo.

Maybe We Can Fool God

When a transwoman
is murdered
no one cares,
because we assume
God doesn't either.

Maybe being a transwoman
feels like an endless game
of hide-and-seek with God.

Maybe God only knows us
by our flesh.

Maybe we've made of our God
a wandering man,
with only our birth name
and baby photo.

One who hasn't already measured
the lineage of our selfhood,
maybe He's our fool.

Maybe when
a boy
becomes
a girl,
she fools God.

Fools Him good
so good,
that he wouldn't be able to find her,
wouldn't be able to recognize her
amongst the rest of us sinners.

Trans-Panic

I've heard of men who grip
and gargle foreign, yet
familiar, body parts, then
know not what to make of
their hands, but murder.

Lynching their lovers,
then abandoning their bodies
in unlocked motel rooms.

Trying to kill off
a part of themselves,
that has been left
a whisper.

I once read of a woman
who spilled of herself
a reddish bouquet.

Who was stabbed, so
many times, in her chest
it almost looked as
if someone was
trying to get away
with her heart.

She was found
with duct tape
over her mouth
so she wouldn't
be able to tell
the whole story,
or, the love
story.

I know trauma
uses silence
as a survival mechanism.

Don't come inside me looking for nothing.

Fire

I've lost
all my favorite toys,
bleached my favorite browns,
and stained my only whites.

I like suffering and suffocating,
my tears know patterns on my face
they are not, yet, ready to unlearn.

Sometimes my scars cough dirt
from their lungs,
my stitches come undone.

I don't know if my skin
was made for getting comfortable with.
I don't know if it grows old
or softens in the sunset.

My mirrors know their place.
My place hasn't been shaved
or apologized to since last vacant.

Didn't Feel Like Winning

She remembers
fighting for her virginity
and winning.

She didn't feel like she won.
She has to remind herself,
when she is alone, that she did win.

The nights she can't sleep
she stays up
counting the girls
who didn't win.

Those girls don't have faces.
They are footnotes
relapsing in the margins
of poems.

They are the dust collected
between the bottom of the curtain
and the stage.
They are whispers.

You never met
these girls,

But you know
all of them.

She Doesn't Look Like Rape

It's not rape if you stay
until it's over.

It's not rape
if you don't scream,
how is he supposed to know
that she doesn't like it
if she doesn't scream.

And if she does scream,
doesn't that mean
she wants more of it?

She will not call it rape
because she made it home
in time to act like it didn't happen.

Because rape doesn't buy you dinner first,
because she don't look like no "rape,"
Because the house was nice,
because her classmates were downstairs.

How she gon' come
back in the kitchen
with all of herself unraveled?

How dare she say no?
How selfish of her

to burden them
with her own trauma?

How dare she tread
so carelessly
in her own darkness?
There is no place for her
to mourn herself,
so she won't.

She will not call it rape
because she doesn't know
how to describe it.

She'll say it was quick,
but really slow,
she will not remember
at which point she earned it.
She wanted it,
until she didn't.

How do you know it was rape
if you choose to bury it?

How do you know it happened
if you don't remember it?

How do you know it was him
if you kept your eyes closed?

She'll realize
the worst part of surviving
is surviving.
She will not call it rape
because she'll have to admit
she wasn't prepared
to fight off a man
from the inside out.

She will not call it rape
because no good
has ever come to a woman
who's claimed
to have seen a monster,
who's ran naked from a monster
in the middle of the night.

So she'll lie there
until it's over
she won't cry,
because crying
will make it all real
and this isn't real.

She won't call it rape
because she knows her body
can handle this type of pain.
She will rewrite the story
before it's even over.

You will not call yourself a _____
because her body was made
for you,
and how dare she
act like
she owns herself.

They Don't Know Anything

Men around me talk about rape like they know, for a fact, that if a man ever forced himself on me, I'd fight like Xena the Warrior Princess. They think I'd kill my perpetrator and bring his body back to the villagers, as a bloody example. Men around me believe that I'll superhero myself out of rape. The men around me think I can fly. The men around me talk about rape as if I'm just too smart to lose something from the inside. They speak so lazy about rape. Men around me compliment me for not being raped. Men around me compliment me for not telling them I've been raped. Men around me think that for a woman to be raped, she had to have been caught, somewhere, being less of herself.

Not, still, all of herself

and, still, broken into.

I exchange body parts
for memories,
this is how I negotiate
myself.

she be acting
like she don't care
'bout what happens
to herself,
like she already went
missing,
and found her way
back home
before anybody
ever noticed.

Who Am I to Blame Her

I know
she is more
of an addict
than a mother,
a lady,
or a woman.

Or maybe
I know nothing.

Maybe
she's all
these things.
Maybe one
has made
her another.
Maybe
she had to become
all of those things
to exist,
so long,
in such a world.

And who am I
to judge her
for all the things
she had to become
in order to stay?

Mind in Gallivant

I met a girl who walked
down Broad and Market
looking for her memories.

Who tried to cut her
memories out of
herself, but never
carved exactly where
the pain was.

Another, who had been
digging for her
memories for so long,
when she stopped, she
didn't know if she was
supposed to lay the
body, or the seed.

I know a woman
who gathered her
memories like old
gold, and pawned
them for new
memories and
never talked about
jewelry again.

Mortality and Magic

Sometimes
your heroes die
and you realize
mortality and magic
occupy the same space.

Whitney: Fairy Godmother

My fairy godmother
left today,
took up her wings,
and fluttered away.

Heard the Holy Ghost,
hummed a note
that rang in her soul.

Made us believe
there was really
something special
about a Christmas Eve
right in the middle
of the ghetto.

"There may not
be anything
under this tree,
No gifts
from three kings
But . . . boy,
can that girl sang!"

Holding notes
as strong as

wooden Baptist
church pews,

With back pockets holding
the Bibles and sins of
some men, who would
scurry away but find
an early Sunday
morning to come back
for them.

Chasing a sound that
could turn a pumpkin
into a chariot.

Made us believe
Cinderella could be a
brown girl,
with a chance at forever
if she had a little faith
and measuring tape,
a little glitter, and
a whisper that
could grant you
one last wish, or a
last kiss.

God placed you in the
dreams of every brown girl,
with a fairy tale in her heart

and a prayer stumbling up
the stairs of her throat.

A Black girl
with faith as blind
as the wind,
yet as real
as its whisper.

Whitney: "Boy, Can That Girl Sang"

Whitney sings
Porgy and Bess
at the 21st American
Music Awards.

It is 1994,
and her voice
is a solo ceremony,
filling her chest
with enough breath
to wind a fire.

She sits on an octave
past heaven.

The rush of the saxophone lags
behind her falsetto,
as if it were a lazy lover.

A choir of collateral, left by
Jesus. Enough voice to stretch
across the Pacific or the ghetto, it
all holding
the same range.

Alone, still the body
of her own symphony.

"Ain't nobody sang like that girl,
that girl sangs like she knows
two Gods, or like two Gods
know her."

The under bark of the tree
that raises concrete.
The moment saxophone
met gospel, and gospel
met its own stuttering
two feet.

The sound of a star falling aimlessly
towards concrete.

The edge of the ocean spilling off
the earth, like a slow sip, into its
own resounding nowhere.

Singing us the name of our God.

Whitney transitions to
"You're Gonna Love Me,"

her voice, a crying
stream, that wails,
"no, no, no wait!"

She bows, debutante of her
own grace. A Christian

girl, with a voice of many
loose tongues.

The saxophone
mellows constant—
like the breeze
of a steady
shadow.

The audience applauds,
and we will remember her
always.

Whitney: Gone

She searches for her voice
in the bottom of her bathtub,
it drowned, a few and a half
years before she did.

The choir makes whisper
of her squanderings.
They speak of what
they would've done
with such favor,
and beauty.

She'd be a woman
to know two deaths.

Whitney: Hologram

The Whitney Houston Hologram
goes on tour in April 2020.

A live band
accompanies a woman
who is not there,
like pallbearers.

Black body still
under contract.

Reactivate a dead woman's
social media, promote.

You don't have to be alive
to make a living,
or a killing.

Aren't we Godly
in our ability
to reincarnate the dead,
magical in our attempt
to falsify falsetto?

Criminal in our ability
to steal the song
right out the casket.

Make her irresistible,
Undying.
More realistic
than she ever was
in her living,
stuck alive,
unresting,
always available.

We stand at her grave
and demand an encore
forcing her
into a Godless resurrection.

This is not Whitney,
just the greatest hits.

This Whitney does not age a bit,
voice left in perfect pitch.

Too good to let go,
too good to get over,
too good to give to God,

They don't give our bodies back to God.

Whitney,
our most favorite tragedy.

They never asked you

if you wanted to sing again.
Gave you the second chance at life
did you a favor,
saved your career,
just not you.

Witch

Does black girl magic really mean,

"look at how that black girl hasn't died yet"

and when she does die,
what does she become,
human?

Sharp

Who taught us,
Black girls,
how to be so sharp
with one another?

4 Inches After 5

Time
is a Black girl
tapping her red,
4-inch
nails, against
a mahogany
kitchen table
on Springfield Ave.

Impatiently,
always
waiting.

I Used to Know Her

Her eyes were not the same
after her husband passed.

Her hair thinned
like a dandelion
in an early wind.

The whites around
her eyes moved
on, as did her
smile.

The refrigerator smelled of a depressive spoil.
Uncertain of what held the most heavy,
the sadness or the fat that faithfull-ed her belly.

She let herself go, and her children.
Long before the babies could memorize the teachings.
I remember who she was. I know her heart to be a damp
place, still fertile, but unbecoming, and it weathered
as so. I don't want to speak of her this way, this woman
I once knew. But to not speak of her this way would mean
not to speak of her at all.

I don't know what's worse, her waiting
to die, or just not waiting for nothing,
nothing at all.

Babies at the Border

We wonder
if babies cry
in their native language.

If they even have a native tongue
to surrender, to the armed men.

These children
do not know America,
but they do know
it doesn't belong to them.

They don't know
why people hate,
but they know hate is cold,
colored in red, it growls,
snatches, and drools,
from its hungry parts.

One child fears
he will be eaten
because things in cages
are to be eaten.

Another doesn't cry
as if he knows the water
will be needed
for much worse than this.

A mother breastfeeds her son
through a metal fence, while his father
holds the back of his head
on the other side.

She pushes her right breast
through a square,
until her nipple pokes out
of the male-female barrier,
meeting the lips of her baby.

The baby reaches for her hand
and other body parts, the parts
that belonged, usually, to him
before the cages.

This baby, eyes closed,
breast in mouth,
reaches

just far enough for him
to know her as mother,

but not enough
to know this
as his country.

The Ocean's Debt

My momma stood
at the edge of the ocean
and played the picket
with Poseidon.

She cashed in
all her scratch-offs,
the ones she was saving
for a rainy day.

So, this morning, when
she saw the water,
she claimed it.

She asked for each
of her children back,
the ones from the ships,
the hurricanes,
and the drownings.
The ones pushed over
the edge.
She called out
each of our birth names,
one by one.

The ones she screamed
before the forced baptismal.

Never,
Never did she forget us.

The Little Mermaid

On July 3, 2019, social media erupted into an uproar regarding Halle Bailey, a Black girl, being cast as Ariel in the next live-action adaptation of The Little Mermaid.

When they tell
the Black girl
she can't play mermaid

ask them,

what their people know
about holding their breath
underwater.

About giving their bodies
to the current,
about all the things
that float.

Ask them about the girls
who lost their mothers,
and mother's tongues
under the sea.

And the danger
awaiting the stillness,
how there's always

something living,
and how there's always
something dying.

There are mothers here.

Mothers who know grief
but have seen it too often
to give it such a name.

She was present for her undressing
but not her unmaking.

Fascinations

Tell me, what do you
want with my ashes, my
hair, my hip bones, my
breast, my
bone marrow?

Speak to me
of your barbaric
fascination
with my skin.

How much am I worth
in your sheets, atop
your altar, on your
auction block?

Bodies Lost in History

I didn't consider all of the female body parts lost in our history, all the names of women, unconsidered. Though I am glad that my questions have led me to many discoveries, I'm deeply saddened by how this truth has materialized in my head, and on these pages. I sit here today, in a café in Newark, New Jersey, thinking about the mentally ill women whose skulls were cracked open in the name of scientific experimentation. I know nothing of this type of pain.

My heart sits heavy thinking about the women who could not run out of their hospital rooms, the women who lay paralyzed, waiting to heal, or to die. And for that woman, who lay waiting to heal, who was her God?

There are thousands of mentally ill Black women in unmarked graves right beneath us. There are girls documented as "women," never considered "girls." Please understand that parts of my body hold rage in their honor. There is no peace in these stories. Time does not breed peace for these stories. Poems do not breed peace for these stories.

I couldn't find all of the names, it's impossible, as is the sum. But, may we never forget the women who didn't get proper burials. Women whose bodies and body parts were stolen and sent to great American universities, like

Johns Hopkins and Harvard, as cadavers. Please remember the bodies that were considered more as chattel, than as daughter. May their memories swell in our hearts. May their stories teach us to honor our own bodies, and to fight for the bodies of our sisters and mothers.

There is no ledger, or official count, of all the women sterilized by licensed American doctors.

Refrain:
Ledger of Women Patients
Sterilized Without Consent

Lucille Schreiber,
17 years old,
white woman,
admitted for mental health,
forced removal of fallopian tubes;

Fannie Lou Hamer,
44 years old,
Negro,
admitted for minor procedure,
forced removal of uterus;

Mary Alice Relf,
12 years old,
Negro,
admitted for inoculations,
forced Depo-Provera injection;

Minnie Lee Relf,
14 years old,
Negro,
admitted for inoculations,
forced Depo-Provera injection;

Katie Relf,
17 years old,
Negro,
admitted for unknown,
forced IUD insertion;

Carrie Elizabeth Buck,
17 years old,
white,
admitted for "feeblemindedness,"
forced compulsory salpingectomy,
inmate note: admitted after pregnancy from rape;

Doris Buck,
21 years old,
white,
admitted for appendicitis,
forced compulsory salpingectomy;

Linda Spitler,
15 years old,
white,
admitted for appendix removal,
forced tubal ligation,
notes: admitted somewhat retarded; promiscuous
    nature;

Anonymous woman #1,
age unknown,

Native American: Cheyenne,
admitted for emergency appendectomy,
forced sterilization,
notes: patient remains anonymous to secure tribal safety;

Anonymous woman #2,
age unknown,
Native American: Cheyenne,
admitted for emergency appendectomy,
forced sterilization,
notes: patient remains anonymous to secure tribal safety.

The Black Stork

Was unkept by any family
a nuisance to my own self,
barely wanted to be touched
or looked at
by any head doctor.

Had outbursts
of no embarrassment
to myself.

A foster child
of unusual nature.

Wasn't the kind of girl
you'd leave in public.
Either you prop me up dead
or put me away
somewhere.

Undaughtered at eleven.
Didn't belong to noooobody,
and nobody belonged to me either.
Got used to all the homes,
Never the hospitals.

Doctors called me headsick,
manic, patient of my own hysteria

suspected mental deficiency,
crazy.

You could do anything
you wanted
with a crazy woman.

Could take anything
from a crazy woman.

Could take all my clothes
and give me new clothes.

Could take all my homes
and give me new homes,
six new homes.

Took my fallopian tubes
right out my body.

Didn't give me new ones tho.

Didn't ask me
if they could have them
for themselves, just took 'em.

Now what's a white man gon'
do with my woman tubes?

Didn't even tell me
where they put them.

Been looking for them
since 1941,
in all of the reds
I could find.

Tore that hospital apart
from top to bottom
looking for my woman parts,
the parts they took from me.

I told myself
as soon as I get my hands
on my woman parts again
I would put them back,
ain't need nobody help.

I'd stuff myself whole again.
I'd stuff myself woman again.
Have myself a chance
to bear children,
and be somebody's mother.

Treated me like a crazy girl
ain't got no kind of memory
like they were punishing my body
for the crazy already in my head.
Like "crazy girl" won't remember
what has been taken from her.

They wouldn't have taken
a white woman's body parts.

Would've left her whole
to pass away like a human,
would've given her peace lilies
and prayers,
would've given her body
back to God.

They didn't give
our bodies back
to God.

They took 'em.

Swine

Wonder what them white folks
did with all the body parts
they stole from us brown folk?

I'm sure there's enough to dress
a museum.

Wonder if they hang them
in slaughterhouses
like salted swine.

HeLa

Tested, and held on to her,
long after she was dead.

Marveled at how
the Negro girl's cells
could multiply themselves
like wild ivy.

In a constant mutation of self.
Dead, but still of plenty,
still of service, still breeding.

They stare at how brilliantly
her cancer can propagate,
taking baby steps
without parent cell.

What else were you to do
with a dying miracle? Huh?
Like a star fell out the sky,
and right on to your lap.
Whatchu gon' do? Throw it
back to God or keep it, huh?

A Pouring Thing

She said her bladder
was as good as a loose fist
after her first baby.

Couldn't hold any
of the water
it poured from her
like a bleeding river.

Slave women, back then,
ain't get to see good good doctors;
either they got better,
or spoiled rotten like dirty women.

And ain't no good use
For a rotten, dirty, woman.

Her first baby dropped
when she was 18.

Pelvis too small to push
that baby through,
like her body already knew
to refuse its becomings
or would-be's.

She aged fast after that.

The pain hated her
just as much
as she hated it.

She bled
of a slave's disease,
and we all knew it,
that the fault
wasn't hers,
just the body.

The doctor came
and claimed her.

Took her for free
said he'd fix her up,
built her up some quarters
in his own yard.

She was awake
and on her knees
for some of the surgeries.

Screamed like a cow in labor,
or like a woman in dying,
naked and open,
nipples hardened
towards the ground,
stomach bloated,
almost stuck, a crying,
pouring thing.

Watching pieces of herself
fall onto a wooden table
like autumn.

The other doctors
watched, took turns
inserting fingers
and scalpels inside of her.
A different kind of molestation.

Slave women weren't allowed
to claim themselves,
or demand
that you treat them like ladies.

Butt perched up
towards the ceiling,
or to the heavens,
held down,
from wrists to ankles.

Tearing her nails
through our flesh,
our sweat
becoming each other's.

It didn't make her
a strong woman,
it just reminded
her that she wasn't one.

A lady.

Doctor soaked up
her urine and blood
with the same sponge
as if it all came from the same place
or was of the same kinda thing.

The sponge swelled
of fresh death.

Her blood reached itself
into every corner of the room
like plague,
or permanence.

She could've died right then
and would've been fine with it.
Thought it to be the only way
to escape her own mangled body,
the body she was forced to have.

It was more broken
when he finished.
She was an 18-year-old
dying thing.
Still having to carry a body
that he made expire on her.

Her slave body.
Her slave girl body.

Her slave girl mother body.
Doctor said she had no pain
but she felt everything.

He went on to cure
a whole lot of white women,
those women
always treated
like ladies.

Mourning

The doctor
blamed her
for the graveyard
her body
had made of itself.

But even it knew
when to mourn.

Girlish

She was a mother,
before she was a woman.

Birthing Babies Not Her Own

The slave women
were checked
for "soundness,"

their ability
to reproduce,
and widen
themselves
like chattel,

their bodies
will host babies
that aren't their own,
but are of them,
in complexion, blood,
and blues,

the Black girl's
body will ripen
before the white one's,

"This Negro woman
can produce
up to eight
Negro babies,"
he says.

Not all will make it
through her,
some will be torn
from her,
some will be buried
in places she'll only see
in her own nighttime,

she will name each of them,
and repeat their names
long after they get new ones,

she will make up stories
of their freedom(s),
make them up unburdened
and unburied,

imagine all her babies
tall, and in shades of green,
fistfuls of flowers,
struts that take on
the wind's rhythm,

and smiles,
smiles that could run their way
across a moon's chest,
imagined they all learned to read
Bible words,
and how to repeat the Lord's Prayer.

They never saw her again,
but she imagined
if they ever did,
they'd know her,
and she'd be a mother,

their mother,
again.

A Friendly Death

Black women are still
gracious enough to not die
out loud.

Crazy

Are women labeled
crazy when you feel
like their rage
outweighs the evidence
of their pain?

Sleep Patterns

I've died in your arms
and shook myself awake
because I didn't trust
where you'd put my
parts.

Mud Pies

If you go looking for dirt,
you will eventually create it.

She's Waiting for Me

That girl you're holding,
she doesn't belong to you.

I know she's unraveled on you
with a childish curl pattern
and restless tattoos.

She speaks like she's got forever
on her breath, but it's bourbon
and weed.

She's waiting for someone,
and my flight has been delayed
for some time now.

And sometimes she doesn't think
I'm coming home.

She gets lonely and confused,
and sometimes your touch feels like mine
but you'd be a fool to love her.

Don't leave fingerprints
or voice mails, or poems.
Just hold her steady
until I make it there.

Where Home Is

You will make her cum,
I'll make her come home.

1,000 Questions on Gender Roles
for a Lesbian

Who's the boy?
Who's the girl?
Who turned who out?
How do you know this isn't a phase?
Who's the top?
Who's the bottom?

When you hold hands,
whose hand is in the front,
and whose hand is in the back?

Who opens the door on a date?
Who pays for dinner?
If you want to get engaged,
who will propose to who?

Who walks down the aisle first?
Who stands at the altar?
How are you going to have a baby?
Which one of you is going to give birth?
What will you do when your child finally
notices that they have two moms?

How do you have sex?
Is sex better, you know—because you—
both have the same parts?

Do you take turns licking each other?
How do you scissor?
When you scissor do you feel anything?
How would you feel anything from rubbing vaginas?

Who wears the strap on?
Do you share the strap on?
What size is it?
Did you pick it out together?
Wouldn't it be easier to fuck a man?

Are fingers really better than dick?
Have you ever had dick before?
Do you ever miss the dick?

God has a wraparound porch
and a sweet tooth.

Invite Me

I met a girl
who holds me
like she is fighting
for me
in her sleep.

If you ever decide to age,
love, invite me.
I'll retire my bones
to make you tea,
and read you poetry.

I know she's having a bad dream
when she grinds her teeth.
She always finds my body
in her sleep.

For the nights I can't
pick you up off the floor,
we'll build a fort.

My body was made for you
to sleep inside of,
you make me want
to straighten things up
around here.

She may be in your sheets, but I exist in your muscle memory.

I've mumbled
between your thighs,
and made up languages
while inside of you.

She doesn't masturbate,
or have sex enough.
I wonder,
where she hides the sticky parts
of her womanhood.

The Light

Stared at a picture
of Dorothy Dandridge
and Harry Belafonte,
wondered if we still
fight the same,
or bite the same.

If they ever made more love
than sense,
if they ever stared
at our generation and wondered
where all the fireflies went,

did they all die
or did they not find us
worth the light?

Did they not find us worthy
of them dressing to the nines
in their shine
waiting to become fallen stars
between the hands
of a blushing girl,
in front of another,
waiting to give up
her audacity,
and her world.

I promise you,
if I died tonight
in these sheets
I would still
want you next to me.

Like this love survived
all of those riots,
I know when you are scared,
I held your hand
when the hurricane came,

pass me my lighter,
I'm sorry I made you cry,
I don't give a fuck if you cry,
I will always wipe your tears
when you cry.

And, I know you did not
give me permission to
but I already started asking God
about you.

I told Him
if He doesn't mind
I'd like to make it to heaven
before you do.

To run your bathwater,
to make you a plate,

to turn the TV
to your favorite channel,
and turn it off,
and make you believe
you left it that way.

And I vow
to never open the door
for a scent other than yours,
and I promise to always remember
your scent,
and that we'll laugh
at everything that hurt
when we were humans,
like when we were poor,
when we slept
on our bedroom floor
on Leslie Street,
when we only had water
and grilled cheese,
the moment you said,
"baby, I may not have any money,
but I got a soft spot, and a melody,
and a pair of arms that can rock you to sleep
so, what, you thinking about taking a chance
on me?"

Love me like you are not waiting for my apology.

You can't break a heart that already came in pieces.

Do you know
how many people
I lied to
to lay
here?

Kill that Nigga Dead

Chile, if you gon' marry that man,
go on ahead and marry him,
but keep yah money
separate.

Don't let no man control you,
or your hard-earned money.
If he got your money,
he got you.

If you gon' marry him,
go on ahead and marry him,
but you be ready to leave him
if he brings you any kind of harm.

Learn his ways, and watch him good,
see if his ways change.
Don't let that man pull at your peace.
Yah peace is all you got.

If you gon' marry him,
marry him, but be ready to kill him.
Kill him dead if he tries
at your body, or your head.

Don't let him try you.

Only then you ain't no slave.
If you gon' marry him,
marry him,
but you ain't gon' be nobody's
slave.

Giving Up God

I was going
to adopt all of your pain,
give them all names
just to have you
to love you.

All the mornings
you didn't want anything
to do with this world,
I would've
given up
mine too.

I would've
given up
my God
for you.

I gave up
my God
for you.

Didn't pray
for 269 days,
replaced Him
with you.

Didn't even miss Him,
didn't even notice
He was gone.

Conversations

I'm just tired
of fighting you,
every week we fight.

Have you realized
We can't go a week
without fighting?

If my momma hear us
you gonna have to leave,
and she ain't gonna want you
to come back.

I don't care
if you don't
come back,
I mean
I care
if you don't
come back.

You just can't stay here
no more.

She don't think
you good for me

no more,
I don't think you good
for me
no more.

Stop screaming at me,
you talk to me
like I'm some bitch
off the street,
you didn't call me one
but I act like one,
what is acting like one?

You make me act like one.
You act
like I'm not on your side,
I'm here,
I'm always here.
I thought
that was the problem
that I'm always fucking here,
with you, the problem
is with you.

We say the same shit,
every week.
Every week,
we say the same shit.
Last time,

was the last time.
Every time
is going to be different.

Why we never try harder?
Or why we never try harder
at the same time?

Or why we never try harder
long enough, at the same time,
to call this an actual fucking relationship?

I do believe
this is an actual fucking relationship,
your mother doesn't believe
this is an actual fucking relationship.

She doesn't even look at me.
Look at me!

I am insecure,
I don't trust you,
you don't even trust you!

Yes, I am laughing
because this shit is silly
and sick, and stupid!
If you love me

why do you make me
look so stupid?

I don't want this to be normal,

I can't tell if this is normal,
this doesn't feel normal,
this is too painful to be normal,
my friends don't think I'm acting normal.

I can't tell my friends about us,
I don't tell my friends about us.

They think I sound crazy,
no one is ever going to believe
you made me crazy.
Don't even know
if one can make another crazy.

I'm not strong
enough
to stop you
from hurting me.

I don't try hard
enough
to stop you
from hurting me.

I don't leave

when you hurt me.
I should've left
when you started
hurting me.

I just thought you'd stop
hurting me.

Thought I could teach you
to stop hurting me,

Thought I could love you
from hurting me.

Dear Ex Lover

Dear ex lover,
I promise
I'll stop chasing
your memories in my dreams.
I'll stop bringing your name up
over cups of coffee, muffins,
and loneliness.

I'll marry a man and lay my heart
on his chest like red roses
on mahogany caskets,
and I'll have his daughter.

She'll have eyes reminding me
God still believes in second chances.
If she ever falls in love with a woman
I'll love bravery down her spine.

I'll be reminded of all the times
we loved like there were expiration dates
tattooed on our inner thighs.

I'll tell her to watch out
For women whose silhouettes
remind her of roadblocks.

To run when she kisses dead skin
that reminds her of dead ends.

If she ever comes home
with eyelids like cracking levees,
bruised kneecaps, and a heart full
of question marks,
I will hold her
like my mother never held me.

I'll clasp her face in my palms
like the New Testament on Judgment Day.
I will remind her that true love
is the passion that allows you
to do the right thing.

And no human is strong enough
to play coaster
to a half-empty heart.

Dear ex lover,
if my daughter ever feels
like she's alone,
as if her heart
isn't a hand-me-down fabric
pulled out of the depths
of her mommy's closet,

I'll remember your name,
and mumble it under my breath.
When she asks me, what did I say

I'll tell her,
"I know what it feels like

to drag a woman out of a cold war,
then being too worn to clean up
the battlefield it has made of you."

I will tell her,
"Your heartbeat sounded like gun shells
tripping over battered cement."

I will tell her,
I know what it feels like
to just want someone to remember you.

And apologies are like oxygen masks
on hijacked planes,
forgive yourself,
before you dare
forgive the person
lying next to you.

I will tell her,
Never regret loving in permanent ink,
scars only give your stretch marks
something to gossip about,
stop signs and hearts are fraternal
twins lost in the pits of open roads
and hollow chests.

Dear ex lover,
if my daughter's mirror

ever looks unfamiliar,
if she is ever too prideful,
and embarrassed
to run in her mother's arms

I will pray she has friends with hearts
filled with thousands of fireflies
who are not too cool to pray with her,
who will tell her to stop looking for light
at the end of the tunnel
and to find God in the darkness.

If she ever falls in love with a woman,
and walks in my house like shattering glass,
and wants to forget everything,
if she ever wants to write off true love,
as simply an experiment,

I won't allow her
to make the same mistake I did.
I will tell her about you.

I will tell her
that we hurt,
and we cried,
and we laughed,
and we smiled.

We smiled like our smiles

were the only smiles
that mattered in this world.

And we fought.

We fought like women,
who loved women,
who loved people,
that didn't love us.

Dear ex lover,
I hope my daughter
never knows
what a goodbye kiss feels like.

I hope she never knows
what "I'll see you later"
really means.

I hope she never memorizes
the dial tone after a last conversation.

Because a broken heart
feels like poisoned butterflies
taking their last flutters
right in the pit of your stomach.

There's no poem for you here.

Monologue: Mother Yells at (Insert Name of Black Girl Here)

ACT I SCENE 1

(Mother rants at child in the kitchen. Daughter sits at wooden table while her mother stands. Preoccupied with dinner, she stops, sporadically, to look her daughter in the eyes while she speaks. Daughter does not speak. She gives girlish nods.)

MOTHER: Don't you know
these white folks ain't gotta
    listen to you?
Ain't gotta tolerate you?
Don't gotta like you?
Don't gotta respect you?

(pause)

They don't gotta make sure you make it
    home to me.
They don't care that you got a family or a
    mother to come home to.
You think these cops care about me?
They don't care about me, (insert name of
    Black daughter)!
Don't you get it?

(MOTHER taps wooden spoon on table. MOTHER gives rage.)

MOTHER: You starting to think you're worth
                something? Huh, chile?
             You starting to think that you won't die?
             Starting to think that they won't hurt you?
             You ain't nothin' but a big fool,
             a big dumb fool.

             They ain't scared to kill you, (insert name
                of Black daughter).
             Is that what you want?
             To be killed?

             You foolish enough to think that . . .
             You can talk yourself out of your own
                death?
             You wanna die?
             You want me to have to come looking for
                you? You want me to get a call about
                you?

(MOTHER stops cooking to walk closer to child, she waves spoon in her face.)

MOTHER: You wanna show some officer you smarter
                than him?
             That's what this about?

That's what you want?
To prove that you are smarter?
You wanna die for being smarter, (insert
    name of Black daughter)?
You wanna die because you didn't know
    when to stop,
when to close your fuckin' mouth!
You never know when to stop!
You don't know how far is too far.

They gon' kill yo' black ass. Just wait,
keep playing wit them police.
Ya hear?
They gon' get you.
Gon' get you good.
And I won't be able to protect you!
Do you hear me?
That mouth gon' get you
in a whole heap of trouble
that your ass won't be able to get you
    out of.

You think it's funny.
It's not funny!
You got one more time, girl, next time you
    won't be so lucky.
Ya hear?

(end scene)

Sandra's Haiku

There was a hanging.
Your fingerprints weren't there.
You were not either.

Image Description

Sandra Bland wearing orange undershirt, and orange V-neck shirt (overshirt). Bland's dreadlocks are short and hang backwards, some fluttering out of direction. Caramel-skinned African American woman. Nostrils widened, nose a reddish brown. She is of tired eyes. Holds head in lazy fashion. Headshot taken against cement wall. Left cheek tightened, eyes express sorrow, or of recent crying. High cheekbones. Brows medium-thin and of a natural arch.

Riddle for a Black Girl

What it to do
for a Black girl
to die today?

May we tell a story,
the riddle,
before it's too late.

May we remember her name
as we repeat her fate.

May we seek her story,
in truth it's told.

May we paint her skin
in a hue of gold.

May we leave her dreads
perfectly intact
May we remember
that she was Black.

May we remember how
she laughed and cried
May we speak
of who she was
before she died.

The Girl Who Didn't Die

Sandra gets her locs done
by Phylicia,
because Phylicia only charges $30,
and uses all-natural products,
you know, the good products.

She started our locs at the same time,
after we cut all the perm out.
We were walking 'round
wit lil twisties in our heads.
She hated our bald-headed stage,
but we were proud and ugly
right at the same time, soul sistas, ha!
I'm just fuckin' around.

We'd sit in the kitchen
smoking and talking shit,
about everything that did matter,
and everything that ain't,
all at once, at the same time,
together.

Every time, the same shit.
The whole place smelled like shea butter,
and there was enough coconut oil
in that big-ass white container
'bove the fridge to grease a newborn,

clean a house,
and cook for an entire family,
and Phylicia did just that,
and then some.

Each comb did something different,
and each one had the story
of the woman before her
between its teeth.

Sandra Bland: A Different Story

She catches the swing of her car door and hops in. She
searches through her blackened leather purse for a pack
of cigarettes, there's always one left in the pack. She
shuffles and realizes that the last cigarette in the pack
belonged to yesterday's routine. The Texas sun is
unforgiving on her leather seats. She drives to the gas
station's convenience store for a fresh pack of 100s. Just
off Tenth and Austin. Drives past the officer who
would've arrested her, misses him by a block and four
minutes. She doesn't die—today.

In the Video Games

If this were a video game
she would've been given a second life,
maybe, even, a third.

Would've been face-to-face
with her intruder.

Would've been able to choose
her own armor
and a weapon of her own
whimsical conjuring.

If shot,
she'd be able to take out her own bullet
without a flinch or scalpel.

Would've watched the wound heal
in a second's swiftness.

Her blood would've reversed itself
back into her body,
as if she'd told it to.
And she'd throw
around a weighty laugh,
while dusting off her shoulders.

If this were a video game
she would've been given a third life,
maybe, even, a fourth.

Refusal

She is not refusing to die,
she is refusing to let you kill her.
She's that kind of stubborn.

She God's Prayer

Tell the Black girl
that all of her prayers matter.
God done seen and heard them all,
stored them in the front of His Levi's,
and washed them deep
into the bottom
of His pants pocket.

Tell her
that she is His favorite,
the part He rereads
for the joy.

She is dark
and never forgotten.

Tell the Black girl,
the ocean and everything
that bleeds, in wet,
belongs to her.

Like I Got Gold Mines

I will prance
in your darkness.
I will be big
and masterful
in my arrival,
swift in my exit.
I will glow, bare fangs
leave a blood trail.

For I am
the Black girl
you cannot kill,

what a thought.

Serena

They will ask you to run,
                  and when you become the fastest
they will fear your lightning,
how it cracks ceilings   and breaks
ground.   They will place rules on your
body,   say it's a distraction from
their game,

                  as if they know better than you
how your bones should wear your own body,
how you should dress up in your own skin.
                  They don't know why your hair
needs extra bobby pins,   or how you got the
    biggest booty in tennis,
something about Compton and collard greens. They will
    not be graceful with your body,
                  but you will always have to be.
When they put you against
                  your own sister,
she'll sharpen you.
                  Passersby will attack your
character,
    Serena smashes racket,
point penalty,
        violation,
                how will she ever come back from this one,
    she is too aggressive,

she has gone too far with her
clothing, how can Serena possibly regroup
from this, fight back,
              women do not yell, women do not take
their shirts off, Serena loses the match and is fined
$17,000,
we cannot allow her to get too out of control.
                        Women are not allowed real emotion
        in tennis,
        in the street,
    in the office,
        in their skin.

        Serena, lean in,
more power, use more power,
    backhand,
back!
    Backhand, Serena!
More!   More follow through!!
    Take the net, Serena,
    be tuff,
    be tuff.

Act like you want to win.
        Forward!
        Forward!
            Back,
            back,
            back,

you got this, Serena,
                net,
                net

        net, Serena,
                yes!
Power, Serena,
play to win!!
                What does it feel like
                        to prepare your body for the
                US Open,
                Australian Open,
                to be cut open.
And to still give them grace,
        even when they call you names,
even when they paint your face,
you give them grace.

Without fear, doubt, or discomfort,
what else is there to overcome?

You're sport,
not spectacle,
        woman before
        competitor.
    When they walk,
        you fly,
when they grunt,
you roar.

You are a fire
catching its breath.
You embrace failure,
never run from it.
We've already
watched you defy
                   gravity,
                         but today,
today, you will become it.

Dear First Lady

For Michelle Obama

Dear First Lady,
I watched as my 4-year-old cousin,
as she sat in the mirror,
placed my grandmother's pearls
around her neck and said,

"Do I look like Michelle Obama?"

This little girl
who does not know how to say
Rice Krispies or macaroni and cheese,
properly said your name
as if it existed in her long list of heroes
in between Snow White and Santa Claus.

My little cousin does not know Jim Crow,
how to interpret the Constitution
or fight for human rights,
she does not know your views
on health care reform,
your Princeton education,
nor can she point to Chicago on a map.

But she knows Black Barbie dolls and nap time,
how to identify your face in a land-field
of misrepresented women

who share our skin color
like a sequin revolution.

She knows your smile, Michelle,
she knows the day
her mother jumped up and down crying,
November 4th's
black and red dresses,
she knows how to say
"African American"
better than her own first name.

You proved that her identity belongs
somewhere in this American dream.
She knows that if she can find your face
in the jumbled channels on television
there's a possibility she can stay up
past her bedtime.

You are everything
her mother never got the chance to be,
CoverGirl's Beauty of the Week,
a love story sprinkled
in an inaugural speech,
a woman
she can mistake for her mommy.

She traded in her Dora the Explorer costume
for a brooch of the American flag,
and a tee shirt with your husband's face on it.

And for the first time
I could identify the revolution
that would actually change the world.
It's not in how many Barack and Martin
comparisons we can make,
but the idea of little boys
jumping off their bunk beds
actually believing that they can fly.

It's in little girls with dreams
and their grandmother's pearls.
My little cousin doesn't know
about the war in Iraq,
she just wonders if Sasha and Malia
like to Hula-Hoop
and if you force them to eat
their Flintstones vitamins too.

Thank you for being
a brown girl's dream come true,
something tangible to look up to.

I know that our skin color
exists on time lines
of women who had craters
engraved in their backs.

Stretch marks similar to maps
of underground railroads.

Grandmothers who couldn't afford
all the ingredients in the American pie.

Women who laid down their lives,
strutted with chips and cracks
in their spines,
dying to inject more estrogen
in "man's kind."

Creating tradition under the idea
that if I can't afford my daughter the world,
a college degree,
or at least, a decent meal tonight,

I'll wrap my grandmother's pearls
around her neck
like a gravity-stricken halo

and I'll whisper in her ear

"Baby,
if I can't,
you will . . .
    . . . she did."

Climbing

Sometimes you speak
like there's something,
or someone,
trying to climb
out of you.

My Sister's Keeper

What does it mean
I keepeth my sister?
That I hold on to her
and love her in ugly,
rotten, and uncertainty.

What does it mean
I keepeth my sister?
That I not abandon her
when she is blind and naked,
exposed to the bare of this world,
the parts that want to break her,
and break her open.

What does it mean
I keepeth my sister?
Even when she don't got no scripture
or 35¢ for stranded calls home.

What does it mean
I keepeth my sister?
Even when all she has is some skin
God gave her
without direction or explanation.

What does it mean
I keepeth my sister?

That I love her
as self
until she finds self.

What does it mean
I keepeth my sister
even when
she don't keep me,
that my tongue holds her
in prayer,
that my hands hold her
in fragility.

Missing Girls

```
J C E X P R B D U D L M T Y G D V Y D V
T C O A C G N A O M I X L O T A W I X I
H V W M D G I W U W B F E L E U R Y E W
R Y X U F L M A D O H R K B R U U K E B
L B C L P O G Z A Q I F T P G I T N Q X
Z J Z D A J R P N I L B A M A F H I H S
Z S A R A Y A T I N Q A I Q M E C Z Q W
M A R Y A M U Y M L N W Z F B O O E J C
H G P K N T Z Q A O E S T H E R D U O A
E H L Q S T C E O P H A R H F W U N E U
Y J Z C F J Q P I H A V W M C U P T W A
D S R C N M F U T A T K L A O K Z L J R
I Z V P U Y D P S U L J I Q E D R L E E
I A T F G N W A A W B P G E D A A C E Z
K F T N N D S L P A O K I I K B A S K I
A A M O F A A I D U P Q H I T R B N R E
R M Y X C V G H L V Z F Y B G M C A I W
R K I R D S Y A B R A A T L Y D I A W V
G U O N O W Y R G M C M N M N I R F M D
A D W Q A P U L M N W N U A H S I A I Z
```

WORD LIST

AISHA	DORCAS	LYDIA	RAHILA
AMINA	ESTHER	MAGRET	RAKIYA
AMINA	FIBI	MARYAMU	RHODA
AWA	GRACE	MODA	RUTH
COMFORT	HAUWA	NAOMI	SARAYA

I've held your daughter
as heavy as a suicide note
on a nightstand.

She said "her God"
won't allow her
to be with me, but
why did "her God"
allow her to fall in love
with me?

Do Not Fall in Love

Do not fall in love
with the Somali girl.
She cannot take you
back to her country.

There is no good word
for "lesbian" in the village
where her father grew up.
Those women lose
their last names.

Her mother prays
for her husband
and the ceremony
of her future.

To love her,
you must love her God,
and to love her God
would mean not to love her,
in that way,
at all.

You touch me like
you've met my body
in a past life.
Can I love you
in a past life?

I Wish You a Lover

I wish you a lover
worth sitting still for.

A lover with an honest memory.
Who won't find you fleeting,
or torn.

I wish you a lover
who won't hold you
after expiration,

a lover who won't watch you
go bad or grow bitter.

A lover more careful
than I was.

I wish you a lover
worth forgiving me for.

Oxygen Mask

Today, I forgave myself
for how I hurt you.
I didn't wait
for your permission.

For if I did,
I'd still be sleeping
next to you.

Reflex

I miss the parts of you
that, reluctantly, get wet
when you want to be shy
and invisible.

Side-Chick Apologetics

If she ever picks up my stench
in your consciousness,
tell her . . .
"I'm sorry."

I never loved a woman enough to let her go when she asked me to.

Scars

I knew a girl
who cut herself,
to escape herself.
She never
escaped herself.

I Was Here

You have lines on your breasts
that make me want to write
"I was here" or
"I won't leave."

Things Left Behind

I'm gone,
but I left
my body
for you.

When You Left, You Left

Sometimes
I think you'll show up
to get your mail.

I wonder where you are
in this world,
if whatever pocket
you sleep in
holds your warmth
and all your stuff.

Is it hard
to sleep
without my body
unraveled next
to yours?

I know
everything is different now,
and all bets are off,
and we loved the best way
we knew how,
but there's still enough food
in the fridge for you.

You Took Sundays

When you left,
so did my memory
of everything
with sugar.

Like French toast,
things that come 10¢
at the corner store,
like Swedish Fish, and
those sour candies
that start off hard,
then melt themselves
sweet on our tongues,
and Sundays.

When you left,
so did every
single
Sunday.

Pac-Man

Maybe Pac-Man,
is a story
about all the endings
you can stomach
in a lifetime.

Path Train

I just thought
we'd have a better goodbye.

When the time came,
we'd wish each other well,
and let the train doors close,
how they always did.

You'd walk away
but then realize
how foolish it would be
to let me go.

Maybe God
was a really good train conductor
in our past life,

Who reopened the train doors
for people who left
really important things behind.

"Always keep 35¢ in your purse to call home if you need something."

—Aunty Boo

God Drives a Chevy

God stands across
the street,
back against
the side of a '66 Chevy,

key still in ignition,
waiting for her
to come outside.

Nola

Instructions: read aloud

She be
gumbo
hot sausage
po' boy
beignets

She be
pralines
ice cups
crab legs
crawfish boil

She be
candy lady
quarter treats
Cajun seasoning

She be
bounce
second line
brass band
2-step
saxophone

She be

front porch
bourbon

She be
Weezy F Baby
Manny Fresh
Magnolia Shorty
Rebirth Brass Band
Big Freedia
Tank and the Bangas

She be
gold teeth
lil baby

She be 107 degrees

She be hurricane
She be alligator
and marshmallow
She be 9th Ward
She be drowning
She be surviving
She be tide

She be spook
She be levee
She be water damaged
She be damp
She be vacant

She be gone
She be back
She be
She be
She be

The 39 Bus Makes Stops in the South Ward

Gloria Brown lives
on South 14th St.,
in the South Ward,
she served
as a lunch lady
at George Washington Carver
Elementary School
before she retired.

At 12 p.m. every day,
she gave Calvin Chambers
an extra milk with his lunch,
because he was my little brother's
best friend, and our next-door neighbor.

She fed Calvin
until he was old enough
to go to high school.

His older brother Al-Tariq
died somewhere
in a high-speed police chase
on his motorcycle.
His funeral was held at Cotton.
Bergen Street stands
like an old man,

who was once an artist,
back in his day,
but has, since, painted his kidneys
a whiskey color.

'Round here,
you don't need to be Muslim
to say *"As-salāmu ʿalaykum,"*

because when you walk
into Kings Restaurant
there will be a 4'11"
Black woman who will ask
for your God, and your order,
and she don't care
if you've made up your mind yet.

You have 10 seconds
to respond . . .

"As-salāmu ʿalaykum, my sister,
I'll go with the catfish,
cheese eggs,
cheese grits,
wheat toast,
with butter and jelly,
and an Uptown please."

I come from a city

that always had enough
home to come home to.

A city that sometimes
only responds
to its Muslim name.

A city that rolls its eyes
and holds its babies tight on the
    27 bus,
because it'll be four more months
before momma gets a new car
so . . .

*"Back door, bus driver,
we got places to go!"*

The Source of Knowledge bookstore
be the only Black bookstore
    downtown
and they'll tell you about Broad St.
before all the white folks got there.

It's Summer 2020
and all of B'Nai and Tyrone's
three Black children
graduated from college.
They keep their degrees
in the china cabinet.

And when they cook
they wear those
"My baby went to a
gooood school" tee shirts.

There's a mother
in the West Ward praying
her child through college,
and sometimes she'll sing it,
and other times she'll scream it,
but that prayer will last her
all of the days of her life.[25]

And the water ain't clean,
but Aunty Joyce is,
and she's been clean
for a minute now,
got an apartment,
and sees her grandbabies
every weekend.

And the Leslie Street
Block Association
still has block parties,
they be a group of old Black folks
who never got too scared
of their grandbabies

---

25. Dominique Christina, "Strange Fruit," *They Are All Me*, 2015.

to celebrate them,
or to pray for them.

So, Ms. Shorter gon' have a cookout,
Uncle Charlie gon' have a cookout,
Keisha gon' have a cookout,
and you ain't gon' worry
about the roaches
because Momma said,

"Everybody better stay in that
room, and I don't want to hear you
breathe, lift a finger,
or move a muscle
until I say so!"

And the street gon' be blocked off
and the city gon' sing,
and Nana gon' listen to trap music
because all of her grandbabies
are in the same backyard
at the same time.

And when the Electric Slide comes on
the people will dance.
And your daddy gon' show up
and bring you your new bike
and promise to never leave.

And Nana,

she made potato salad
and she mixed it
with her whoooooole arm.

And it's gon' be 8 p.m.
until the sun comes up.

So you better stop by now,
stop by,
and come on,
and get you a plate.

There's a Nice Breeze Outside

"The weatherman
says there will be a nice breeze
outside today
so turn off that AC
and open the windows,
let some fresh air in that apartment,
always so damn
stuffy in there."

"I love you too, Daddy."

God Is Watching

She asked me
if I thought
God was watching . . .
"you know, when we kiss?"

"Yes, He is."

Even After

I will love you
even after
you change your mind
about me.

Brown Marks

A lover told me,
she could feel every line,
could follow them
with her fingertips.

Maybe God leaves
stretch marks on women
to direct us home.

973-330-0082

(dial home)

Black Girl, Call Home.

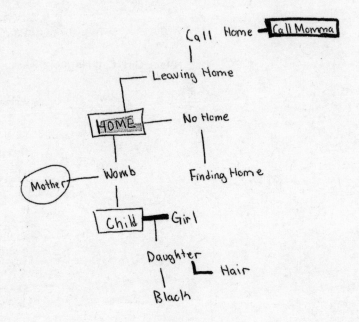

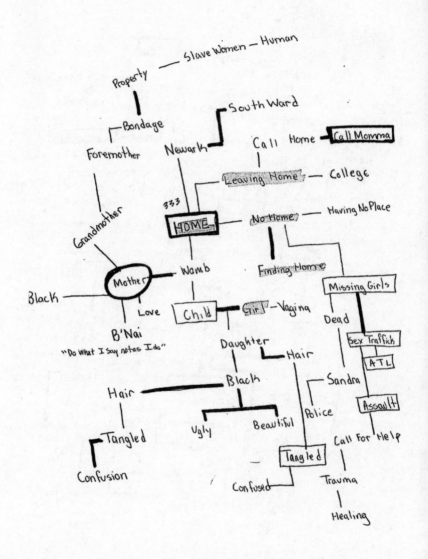

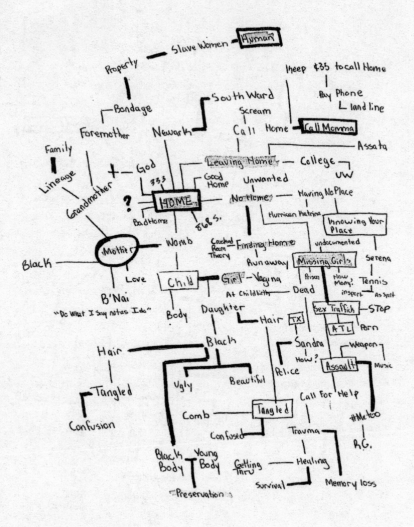

ACKNOWLEDGMENTS

To my family: Mommy and Daddy. My brothers, Tyrone and Antione Mans. My Nana and late Poppa. My aunt Vonnice Hynes, and late uncle Andre Hynes. My cousins Andrea, William, Anya, Alea, Aaliya, Tatianna, Bunny, Jared, Nichelle, Theo, Jordan, Taria, and Taylor. All my aunts, uncles, cousins, friends, and family, given to me, chosen for me, and reimagined with me.

Khajuaan Walker, Sharell Jeffrey, Diona Morgan, Hae-Jin and Jacob Marshall, Assumpta Vitcu, Christina Jackson, Sabrina D. Cates, Renault Verone Africa, thank you for caring for me.

To the men who looked out for me at home, and now in heaven: William "Uncle Bill" Manns, Halim Suliman, Jerry Grant, Shamsuddin Abdul-Hamid, thank you.

Alysia Harris, Zora Howard, Carvens Lissaint, Miles Hodges, Naja Selby Morton, Natalie Lauren Sims, William James Lofton, Avery Sawyer, Thiahera Nurse, Cydney Edwards, Ahlaam Abdul, Adom Hinkle, Nat Isobaker, Niko Tunnmak, Andres Gallardo, Alex Cumming, Valencia Clay, Jennah Bell, Joshua Kissi, Kevin Coval, Dominique Christina, Angel Haze, Adrienne Wheeler, thank you for loving your craft the way you do, your craftsmanship has inspired many a sleepless night.

Thank you to Kamilah Forbes, Ms. Brazell, Gene "No-Malice" Thornton, my college professors: Amaud Johnson and Sandra Adell, and Rafael Casal and Sofia Snow for educating and mentoring me.

Thank you to Morgan Jerkins, Clint Smith, Danez Smith, Jericho Brown, and Maisy Card for being so generous with your support of this collection.

The honorable Mayor Ras J. Baraka, Newark Public Library, New Jersey Performing Arts Center, and Dodge Poetry Festival, your support has been paramount.

Thank you to Busboys and Poets and the Nuyorican Poets Cafe for allowing me to make my first few dollars as a touring poet.

To 3rd Cohort, OMAI First Wave, the University of Wisconsin–Madison, Urban Word NYC, and every Newark poet for every opportunity given, to me, to learn and love poetry.

To the Zeta Xi chapter of Delta Sigma Theta Sorority Inc. and Soror Mary Rose, thank you for teaching me all about sisterhood, love, and the discipline a Black woman would need to survive in spaces and on shelves just like these. Diamond, India, Evett, Dianna, Shawn, Raechel, Ashley, Connie, Precious and Iyanna, Bekah and Selah, I love each of you dearly.

To my sister-friends, Fayemi Shakur, Bimpé Fageyinbo, K. Desireé Milwood, Mia X, Jillian M. Rock, Kween Moore, Antionette Ellis-Williams.

To the women who took a chance on me: Katherine Latshaw, Erin Harris, Jen Monroe; we did it!

Finally, I am eternally grateful to every Black woman writer who came before me, who allowed this journey to be possible. Writers including Alice Walker, Toni Morrison, Maya Angelou, Sonia Sanchez, Nikki Giovanni, Patricia Smith, Audre Lorde, Ntozake Shange, Octavia Butler, Zora Neale Hurston, Gwendolyn Brooks, Lucille Clifton, and many others. This would not have been possible without you, and I am grateful.

And to you, of course, thank you.

AUTHOR'S NOTES

"Period" is written after Dominique Christina.

"South 14th Street: The Attic Window" is an excerpt taken from the poem "Waiting" by Jasmine Mans with Alysia Harris.

"At Aunt Kawee's House in Oklahoma" is inspired by a personal conversation with Natalie Sims on October 10, 2019.

"And Jay-Z Says 'We've Moved Past Kneeling'" refers to Shawn Carter's press conference as reported by Des Beiler, "Jay-Z Defends NFL Partnership as Eric Reid Accuses Him of Helping Bury Kaepernick's Career," *Washington Post*, August 15, 2019, https://www.washing tonpost.com/sports/2019/08/15/jay-z-defends-nfl-partnership -colin-kaepernick-marks-third-anniversary-protest/.

"Didn't Feel Like Winning" is inspired by Carolyn M. West and Kalimah Johnson's "Sexual Violence in the Lives of African American Women," *Applied Research* (March 2013).

"Whitney: 'Boy, Can That Girl Sang'" is inspired by Whitney Houston singing "I Loves You, Porgy" at the twenty-first American Music Awards in 1994.

"Bodies Lost in History" is taken in part from *Medical Apartheid: The Dark History of Medical Experimentation on Black Americans from Colonial Times to the Present* by Harriet A. Washington (New York: Anchor, 2006).

"Image Description" refers to Sandra Bland's mug shot taken at the Waller County Jail on July 10, 2015, in Hempstead, Texas.

"The Girl Who Didn't Die" is written after Patricia Smith and inspired by Alice Walker.

"The 39 Bus Makes Stops in the South Ward" is a poem commissioned by Newark, New Jersey, Mayor Ras Baraka, and the line "all of the days of her life" is borrowed from Dominique Christina's "Strange Fruit" in *They Are All Me* (2015).

THE FOLLOWING POEMS APPEAR IN SOME FORM IN JASMINE MANS'S
CHALK OUTLINES OF SNOW ANGELS:

"Dear Ex Lover"

"Black Son"

"Fire"

"My Sister's Keeper"

Excerpt on page 43 from "How Rose Became Red"

"Dear First Lady"

"Whitney: Fairy Godmother"

"Birmingham"

Excerpt on page 35 from "A Little Girl Died Today—and Her Voice
        Was a Drowning Piano"

Jasmine Mans is a Black American poet and artist from Newark, New Jersey. She graduated from the University of Wisconsin–Madison with a B.A. in African American Studies. Her debut collection of poetry, *Chalk Outlines of Snow Angels*, was published in 2012. Mans is the resident poet at the Newark Public Library. She was a member of the Strivers Row Collective.